DySfUnCtIoNaL PeOpLe

Laura Grace

1. CONTENTS

INTRODUCTION

INTRODUCTION

I'm sitting here thinking how much I want to love people, and how I do love people. We all are so very hard to love sometimes, and it's not always because we are different but quite often it is our differences that seem to separate and divide us.

We use clichés such as "We can agree to disagree," but that isn't always the solution. This morning as I write this, I realize that trying to love people *their way* just took most of my morning. I offered to pray for a person who didn't know what time they might be available for me to say a simple prayer. Other times, their way turns out to not be my way and our worlds seem to collide.

My offering of love has often seemed to turn into some crazy version of gumby, where I bend myself all around, to try and accommodate a person who refuse to settle down and get some boundaries. In a world where intolerance is the accusation of the day, how do we survive this thing called ministry, and help toward those who say they need our assistance?

This book is going to cover some of the types of people I have encountered, a description of their behavior as well as my own dysfunctional behavior at times.

Truly (and you must admit this) interactions with others is one of the hardest obstacles we will ever face in this life. Is it me? Is it you? Who is to blame for this thing called not getting along? We wonder all the time. Should I let go or should I keep trying?

These are questions we ask, and there is not always a simple answer but together we may just find a solution.

A Challenge to Grow....

My hope is, at the very least this book will help you laugh, settle down, find your center, and be able to say, "I'm not alone" It is my hope that you will realize there is truth to be told, and truth to be implemented.

Although Love is the answer, there are times we must realize a big dose of truth helps the plan for love find its' way into our heart to avoid the treachery of burn-out.

With Love,

Laura Grace

1. BOSSY BOSSES

I am starting with this type because I'm sure we've all had one. A bossy boss. What is a bossy boss? Aren't they supposed to be bossy? Well sure, they are, but let's face it, we've all had that over-the-top, gung-ho, never-listens, and always-demands-respect type of bosses. Haven't we?

I noticed as I got older, I had a little more understanding about what it means to be "the boss," partly because of raising children. When I was younger, I was far more likely to take it hard if the boss seemed to be just getting on my case.

There are always those types that listen to no-one and treat us like we are robots who only live to do this job. As an employee of many jobs in my lifetime, I do have to say I feel qualified to talk about this subject.

Unintentional dysfunction

Restaurant work is a unique position, because you have a boss to please and the customers as well. You may find yourself squashed between two opinions, which is how the customer wanted something done and how the boss asked you to do it. There is nothing more stimulating than having your head chewed by both parties, the customer who was supposed to be always right, and the boss whose instructions are law.

I worked as a waitress for a time and was also a dishwasher and fry-cook. I just want to say that there is a big difference between necessary bossiness of bosses and being dysfunctional. Too-busy bosses often are short-tempered, a bit unfair at times, and truly don't mean to be. In other words, it's not personal.

Because I am a writer in the subject of growing, I find it necessary to state the obvious, which is that in our own personal growth from younger person to older adult, we often do realize that what we once considered to be an over-the-top boss, was really a person with too much on their plate and is now coming apart at the seams.

As a dishwasher, someone who shouts, "You need to wash more forks, we are out," is not a ridiculous person. They are just handling the stress of a busy restaurant full of customers who would really like to have some forks.

I was working for a place one time; and was hired to be a waitress, however, the cook did not show up one unforeseen day. The boss summoned me to the kitchen and said,

"Have you ever cooked?"

"No," I said.

'You're going to learn today," He said, without apology.

I was looking at tickets lined up above me and saw one that said, "Hamburger, Fries, MS' and I grabbed a frozen patty.

"Not like that," the boss said, and threw about twenty meat patties onto the grill, handed me the spatula, and walked off to cook the fries.

I learned in a trial by fire that day, and in no way was the boss being mean to me. He simply had a restaurant full of customers, his cook didn't show up, and he used the only tool he had (qualified or not), which was me. I survived the ordeal just fine, with minimal damage concerning the burgers, plus gained another skill in the process.

Mean Bosses

I did have some bosses, that I would say were downright ornery. One that stands out, was at a little booth at the fair where I was hired to sell hot pretzels, drinks, and hot dogs. He ran out of ice, went to get some, and while he was gone I handled the busy booth by myself like a champ. I can still see him roaring into the food trailer and saying, "Empty your purse!"

"What?" I said, (horrified) and he said again,

"Empty your purse, I saw you take money out of the till." I did not take money out of the till, and I was highly insulted. I started to cry at the humiliation of having to empty my purse as customers stood outside the window waiting for pretzels, wondering what crime I must have committed to warrant such a shakedown.

Naturally, there was no money in my purse, other than the five dollars I had with me when I came to work that day. By this point in time, I was in my late twenties, and had seen my share of both good and bad bosses. He offered no apologies for his ridiculous demand that was based on what he thought he saw while driving back with the ice.

I chose not to show up for work the next day, and without notice. Why? Because I did not know how to confront him.

For some reason, I just never learned to do confrontations very well, and had this deep dark fear I would always lose the argument. I was afraid to tell him what a jerk he was, because by now I had learned "How to be a Christian." I remember prior to becoming a Christian, I had no trouble saying what I thought, no matter how harsh it sounded.

Now I had to stop and ask myself if any thoughts I had were loving or kind, and none of them were. So, I did the truly LOVING thing, (and I say this sarcastically) and never came back, giving no notice, and secretly scolding myself for being such a chicken.

Looking back on the incident, I do wish I had said,

"Your shake down and humiliating treatment of me was uncalled for, and since I won't risk you doing something like that again, I will not be back tomorrow."

Being a Christian seemed to complicate this matter for me. Why? Because, I was in a church where the bible studies were constantly centered on the right answer for every situation, and every bit of it came from the bible. I was either supposed to turn my other cheek, meaning let him do it again, or be silent and just pray for them.

This was a three-day job at the fair and not a life time career I was involved in. I think I could have told the truth and then walked out, and God would not have been upset with me, but at that time, I was dysfunctional. You see?

All I could see at the time, was that this man had humiliated me and made me cry in front of a bunch of strangers, and for no good reason other than his own suspicious mind. He was dysfunctional, and so was I

The stories about growing up go on and on. I told my friend that I am going to write a book called Fifty-Five Jobs, because that's about how many I've had if I include the temporary jobs, babysitting, places I didn't stay, places I had to move from, and so on. When I talk about people being dysfunctional, I am by no means leaving myself out of the loop. The question is, are we learning from it all?

The best way to get over someone being a problem, is to realize that we've often been a problem ourselves. Whether we realize it or not, we too have hurt people, let them down, disappointed them fully, and have been oblivious sometimes to our own areas of dysfunction.

Restaurants Again, and Prayer

I do want to say that in most jobs such as restaurants, motels, and other service-oriented positions, the bosses I've had have mostly been nice. They understand serving customers is stressful enough and are often grateful for an employee that shows up on time, stays flexible, and keeps a cheerful attitude. I have a friend who had some picky bosses when she was waitressing and used to go in the bathroom and cry and pray she would make it through her shift at times.

Her story leads me to my biggest answer as to how I got through difficult times with bosses, which is first and foremost, to pray.

Did you ever just pray and ask, "Lord, what should I do about this person, as I want so much to get along with her/him but don't know how really?" And, did you ever pray, and the problem just seemed to get worse? I've had that happen too.

I am a spiritual warrior, so prayer is my number one defense against all enemies, foreign or domestic. I've been to prayer seminars, read books on spiritual warfare, and have been to so many bible studies and read so many Christian books on relationships I have simply lost count.

I've always believed in overcoming, and the best way to do that is to arm myself with good information on how to combat what I'm fighting. However, (and I do wonder if God did not allow me to have so many jobs for the experience itself) It seems as though no matter how much I study, pray, read or arm myself, there is always that situation that never got mentioned in my studies.

A Scary Motel Story

We were running a busy motel, and I was the manager of the place, along with my husband. The boss was coming to stay and let us have two days off, so we were cleaning frantically, and telling the housekeepers to do everything doubly-right. I went and inspected the rooms myself, and made sure every counter, every floor, and every mirror were clean and sparkling.

After a thorough inspection and washing some things over again, I felt I was ready for their arrival.

The bosses showed up, smiled, and told us to have a good time. I remember the husband part of the team said, "Everything looks great," and gave us $100 bonus. The time away was much too short, but I felt ready to face the crazy-busy motel when we came back. I walked into the living quarters of the motel, and was met by the bosses' wife, who had a box of rags in a box and a horrible looking scowl on her face. "We need to talk," she said, and in a stern voice, "Sit down." I sat down.

What followed was a fifteen-minute butt-chewing, where she pulled out a rag with some dirt and said, "I found this in room 112, and I found this in room 116," and on and on it went. By the time she got done, she had me in tears and total humiliation. Add to the humiliation, consternation, confusion, bewilderment, and eventual anger, and I just may have adequately described this incident. I could not for the life of me figure out where she found these streaks of dirt she was waving around on the white rags in her hand.

After she left, the only conclusion we could come to, is she must have used the rags to wipe deep into the recesses of the heat registers or perhaps some was from very high places we failed to reach. My husband has an eagle eye, and he had inspected the rooms, too. I say this with all sincerity, I know we did not deserve what happened that day. I may never know if she did it to keep us from asking for a raise, if she had a screw loose, or if she was super-obsessed with cleaning beyond what is normal.

Later in that job, which lasted over two years, her husband did tell me she was over-the top about cleaning, and she did not come with him after that other than one time. Another thing this boss did to us, is when we were gone on our days off (two days every two or three months) she called me and yelled at me because "my housekeeper' did not show up. Here I was on a badly needed rest, and she is calling me to yell at me over something I could not control.

Finally, I understood why the last managers had taken off in the night, leaving a note on the table with their resignation.

Now I ask, have you ever had a boss just do something completely off-the-wall, making no sense, and you had no clue what to do about it?

I said, "I don't know" In reply to what she should do about the absent employee and was thinking how when the housekeepers did not show up I always had to do the job! I didn't dare say that, although I did think about saying it.

As I already told you, I am a praying woman. This person did not change, and in fact when we were told the motel sold (a little over two years later) which was because the place was showing a notable profit, this boss was still not about to cut us any slack. We had prayed and done what we'd promised, which was to work extra hard to see the business increase. We had done what we promised, however promises were not kept toward us.

We were told the motel sold at the beginning of summer, 2006. My worst fear had happened. When we sold our mobile home to move and take this job; We both knew if we ever lost our job, we could be homeless.

Therefore, I secured a job almost right away, and was told I needed to start in two weeks. I informed the husband of this boss-team that we were leaving in two weeks and could not stay the entire month, as we would need the extra income to be okay financially.

He said, "If you will stay until the new owner arrives, I'll give you one percent of the sale." They lived out of town, and he said the closing would not be for a month, and he really needed us to stay put.

I asked my husband and he said, "Get it in writing.'

I went back to the boss and said, 'We need that in writing.'

He said, 'Oh Laura, that hurts my feelings after all we've been through here, that you would need it in writing." I thought about the bonuses he'd given me, and all the times he had kept his word to us.

Despite my husband's warning, I dropped it as a condition and decided to trust him. A little less than a month later, immediately on closing of the sale, the husband and wife showed up unexpectedly. We were in the process of moving out, but they were early.

When I said, "We didn't have time to clean yet," (as we scrambled to get gone) He said to me, 'That's okay don't worry about it, we came early."

Guess what? When it came time to pay us, he refused to give us the promised one percent, which was about three thousand dollars. My husband was mad, we filed a court claim, and they kept having the venue changed for court until we finally gave up. And why they didn't pay us you wonder? His wife the white-rag lady, said we didn't clean the place and did not deserve the promised reward for staying.

Not all bosses who gave us a hard time, were mean, but some were. Many were frazzled, tired, harried, and many were not even cut out to be a boss, but very few were mean to me. I must say I've had more good bosses than bad.

Advice on Handling Bosses

The biggest and best advice I can give you is, that unless you have an unreasonable boss, try to communicate with them. Choose a time when they are not busy or ask if there is a time you can talk to them. If you're getting to the point where you might quit, list out the things that are bothering you with as much brevity as possible.

If they won't or can't meet with you, write them a letter and keep a copy. I hope you are a praying person, but if you're not, at least stop and ask yourself what is worth losing your job over. A good boss that wants to keep you will be willing to talk, and likely would rather not have to train someone else, unless they truly are forced to.

Your boss may give the impression that you are disposable; and they don't care if you leave, but often that is only a front. Because I went from an employee to a boss myself, I quickly saw how difficult it is to replace lost people. I was willing to drive and go get my housekeeper who had a broken-down car rather than having to clean the rooms myself. I was also willing to give second chances if they would just communicate with me about what obstacles they faced over getting to work on time.

What many do not realize, and what I did not realize, is the things we have in our own history, dysfunction going on in our own homes, and whether we did or did not learn to confront in a healthy way are all added into the equation of our outcome.

Some of us have minor PTSD-like issues, where we are not diagnosed with this condition, but we have reacted badly to a situation because of past experiences. A person with an authoritarian parent that did not allow any arguing and threatened punishment if there was any argument, will probably lack healthy confrontational skills.

The reason I am so passionate about personal growth, is during a five-year period where I prayed and searched my own soul rather than just attending one bible-study after another, I came to see many things about myself that needed to change. When we see we haven't arrived, we continue to grow, and develop more into better people.

I remember thinking the world was coming apart, and I didn't have time to grow. I thought I just needed to get out there and do great things for Jesus. I honestly felt I didn't have time for much self-examination. Besides, didn't God say I was already a "new creature" in him? This verse of scripture is meant to be an encouraging prophecy about what we will become if we stay with him.

It's not an overnight-right-now BAM I-am-changed, kind of thing. I thought it was. No wonder I had so many problems on top of more problems. I was refusing to grow!

The Recompense

The conclusion of this story of the boss who didn't give the one-percent bonus is this:

I was very upset, and so was my husband. I had sold my washer and dryer to take that job, and a reasonably new one at that. I intended to buy a washer and dryer set with part of the money.

I said a prayer, forgave them verbally, and said, "Father I trust you to make things right, in Jesus' name." I then proceeded to do my laundry at the laundromat for several months and every time I got angry about it, I said out loud, "I forgave that, God's got it now."

Six months after we'd been robbed so to speak, a mysterious notice came in the mail that we were getting a check for some money that was some sort of refund check (not from them) For over three-thousand dollars. We bought a washer and dryer with part of the money.

I have noticed every case is different. What caused me to just ask the Lord to pay us back is that first, I already knew unforgiveness and wrath was not good for my own soul. I had learned that the hard way. Second, I heard a testimony one time, just like the one I'm telling you, about a guy who forgave a person who stole a camera from them, and they prayed the way I did, and got another one months later without having to pay for it.

I can't promise you that you will see all justice happen in your lifetime, but I can say that I've seen many times that if I just let a thing go, Things turned out okay in the end.

Some people you can have a talk with and things can get better, while others, such as this person with the dirty rags and who was determined not to pay us; it's better to leave things alone. There are people who will not change no matter what you say to them, no matter how hard you cry, and no amount of physical force will make them comply with your wishes.

Those of us who have a "We can change the world" mentality, will do well to heed that old prayer found in coffee rooms for group meetings across America:

"Lord, Grant me the serenity accept the things I cannot change, courage to change the things I can, and wisdom to know the difference." (Reinhold Niebuhr, date unknown).

This prayer is completely biblical. So often, we just need to accept what we cannot change, and move on to a place where we can truly make a difference. Amen?

"Remind *them* of these things, charging *them* before the Lord not to strive about words to no profit, to the ruin of the hearers." 2 Timothy 2:14 (NKJV).

2. CONTROL-FREAK FRIEDA

To all the people named Freida out there, I apologize. I had to pick a name, this one seemed catchy, and I mean you no harm!

The thing is, Control Freak Freida, Fussy Fred, and Bossy Lucy often have something in common; They want to be in control. We'll focus on Freida, for now.

She drives everyone crazy wanting things done in her preferred way, and she doesn't consider that any way but her way, is the right way. For those who have their own way of doing things, poor Freida, whether she means to or not, will drive them almost crazy!

I knew a gal once, and she had a right way to do things (all the time) and nobody could get a word in edge-wise. Freida comes in all shapes and sizes, and she controls for various reasons. It could be she wants her dinner to look picture-perfect as she saw in a magazine, and if only the food looks good, the table is set right, and all is perfect, then (and only then) her dinner party will be a screaming success. The problem is, Freida is fraught with fears, and the fear is the party will not be successful. She feels the outcome is all a reflection on her, so the control issues just never seem to end.

If you get the right food, the right tablecloth, the right dishes, and the chairs are set just right, and if she knows in advance how many are coming (so all the chairs are in place) and oh, did I forget? Freida needs the right centerpiece, the right candle, and the ambience of the room must be just right. Plans must be made regarding what will happen after dinner, what dessert dishes must be used, and what game or conversation will take place after the meal. At any point in time, if a person does not cooperate with the flow of Freida's plan, they become an instant enemy to the cause, and may be met with angry looks, barking noises, and a whole lot of frustration from Freida!

For these types, it's all common sense. To the person working with her, it may seem like a nightmare from hell itself. Two major virtues or belief systems collide whenever we have Laid-back Lenny and Control-Freak Frieda. Who wins in this situation? Should we have a fight to the death over how a dinner party is run? I don't think so, and neither do you I am guessing. What happens much of the time is Lenny Gives Frieda her way but becomes less and less enthused about dinner parties.

Others who do not know what to say to her, may decide to stop coming to dinner events that seem overly-controlled. Frieda cries because nobody comes anymore, and her family and friends have no idea how to help her calm down.

I've had my control-freak moments myself, and I learned it from Freida. She let me know the right way to do things. I followed her example, but my visitors would not play ball. It just happened that most of my guests were into relaxing, not being on time, and did not do the formal-dinner-party-ideal so well.

The last time I remember getting very upset it was at my children. They were late for dinner and I was stressed out the food was getting cold. There was another time I also stressed out over the meal and now they don't even want me to make dinner anymore. Can I blame them? The last time we got together we went to the restaurant and enjoyed our time visiting versus the traditional dinner-party fiasco where everyone must comply.

Freida's heritage goes way back to a time when dinner parties were the only thing happening that were good in life and it had to be just right, because the most wonderful event they knew was the family gathering. In those times many centered their feasts around harvests, holidays, and celebrations over weddings and other big events.

You remember the feasts they had in medieval times, right? They had no television sets, no movie theatres, and there were some plays or music, usually during the dinner that was a result of hours of work and cooking. These feasts were a production to show off wealth while other times it was for the sheer fun of it. Either way, there are those who are very passionate about dinner parties.

I have put up with control-freak Freida. I did it her way. In the end I thought; "This was a nice party, I want to do it to." I had never taken into consideration that some people don't want turkey, or maybe no pie, or perhaps they like their food cold, or maybe they came to see me, and not necessarily my fancy dinner.

I remember the last time I tried to do a huge dinner in my

little kitchen, and how upset I got over food getting cold and my late but beloved guests. I was so busy fussing it was not fun for them, so in the future, they didn't even want me to cook. I went through some little-kid drama and cried and said to my husband; "They didn't care what I did for them!" I felt so rejected, and I did. I do know to a degree, how Frieda feels when nobody wants to participate, anymore.

I'm not sure when it happened in my life, but I finally realized whatever I judge people for, I have probably at some time done the same thing. I think it came of constantly wanting to learn from my mistakes and seeking God for truth about me, and where I have gone wrong, rather than just praying about the faults of others.

Jesus said we can commit any sin in our heart, without even doing it. When I had murder flash through my heart (even for a moment) as far as He is concerned I committed murder. If I lusted I committed adultery, and if I wanted to control everything my motive was not pure love for those I am serving.

Anything more important than God and his will is out of order with him. If we have got to have things all our way, it's not love, and it's not justice. Control Freak Frieda? I do know who she is. I think we all have a little of Freida in us, but let's not get addicted to having to be in control.

So many people do not realize how soul-wounds are affecting them at times. How we know our soul is healed, is we are no longer touchy. Ever touch a fresh wound where you cut yourself? It hurts. It's the same thing with a soul wound. Touchiness in ourselves helps us to see where the hurt is, and what we need to pinpoint, in prayers for healing.

I've spent a lot of time asking God to heal every single one of them, and I don't just ask I believe for healing. It's something God wants to do for you. He restores my soul, Psalm 23 (NKJV).

A word on Spiritual Warfare

For those who believe in spiritual warfare, yes, you can bind the spirit of control in Jesus' name. You can tell it to stop coming against you, but it won't stop a controlling person from trying to gain control. This is because all evil spirits do is come along and help people be this way the same way the Spirit of God helps people be greater, faster, stronger, and wiser, in something they already want to do.

Just as God by his Spirit equips people to do good works, the devil loves to help people do bad works. Binding the devil will not get rid of the whole entire problem. You are dealing with a person who is dysfunctional. According to my bible, you'll have to see your own faults and not be blind yourself, if you want to lead anyone out of a ditch.

Learning not to Judge

I remember when I used to just bash everyone that was not like me, and went around thinking, "What's wrong with them?" When we don't have the same issues as someone else, it's so very easy to get judgmental. One time I had a person say' "You are judging me, aren't you?" Wow, they nailed me, because I was!

After that, I went through a long period of refusing to even LOOK at anyone's faults for fear I'd judge them which is not healthy either. A good thing is to come to a place where we can see the fault and yet accept them the way they are and love them.

Even if we don't feel loving or kind, we can still behave that way, and try to think of a way to help them out of the pit of having to be in control. Can I be honest with you? Frieda is not having much fun, and neither are her playmates.

Understanding People

People are products of their backgrounds, including their experiences, hurts, impressions and memories. Rarely do they intend to be mean to us, or to ruin our day. It can be very hard to find the balance between being understanding of others, patient and kind, loving and tolerant, and still find the time to grow and go forward ourselves.

Too often, I have found myself in the extreme of enduring a person who seems dysfunctional to the point where I literally have no time to develop and grow myself in the areas God is dealing with me about.

I believe it is for this reason, that people often get categorized as rebellious, unteachable, or some other authoritarian label and get left in the dust to die, while the rest of the church goes forward without them.

We often use scripture to justify leaving people in the dust, when in truth, we need just a little more understanding on how to pray or some insight about how to help them.

Why would we send someone to a psychologist or leave them to falter when we are able to learn to understand them better? This rigid army mentality has got to stop.

I realized that long ago, when I was labeled and left to sink or swim. My pain of feeling misunderstood is what led me to learn about how to give understanding to others about dysfunctional people who are like I was. How is learning to understand people harder than learning to cook a meal without using wheat? Very often, we are more willing to take care of the body than we are a person's soul.

We see the need to feed the hungry, but we give up on a person who needs their soul fed, because they won't go to church with us. Why can't we feed them? Shouldn't we be able to by now? After all, we are all called to minister and to give freely what God has put inside of us. Isn't that right?

There are times a person needs another person to sit by their bed and spoon-feed them some chicken broth for their weary and broken hearts. If Laid-back Lenny tells Frieda she is just a control-freak, how does that help?

Maybe it's time we realize we all have gifts from God within us, and we can use them freely every single day. We do not have to be the pastor to minister to people. We do not even have to have the desire, necessarily, to go out and truly help others.

What we do need, I believe, is an understanding we all are to grow, and this is because we are disciples and not just sheep meant to sit fat and happy in the fold.

I would say all of us probably need to grow into people who are more helpful and less offensive, and hopefully stop making excuses for why we need to write people off just because they don't instantly comply with how we think they should be.

Would we want that done to us? I don't think so.

"And just as you want men to do to you, you also do to them likewise." Luke 6:31 (NKJV)

3. LOFTY LUCY

"The Lord says: "These people come near to me with their mouth and honor me with their lips, but their hearts are far from me. Their worship of me is based on merely human rules they have been taught." Isaiah 29:13 (NIV).

Lofty Lucy wants to know something nobody else knows and to show off her knowledge. She will often study diligently, but not for the sake of personal growth. Lucy is too busy trying to gather information to put others in their place to display just how much she knows.

She is insecure, doesn't feel like she fits in most times, and yet, a part of her really does want to help. Lucy is unaware that most of her tips and input is not-that-helpful. I've been lofty Lucy at times, so I understand her.

Her un-timely and often mis-applied 'advice" leads to frustration on the part of the treasure-seekers that are after God's will for their life. Furthermore, people find themselves clamming up and not wanting to tell her their problems anymore.

Poor Lucy! Because of her insecurity issues, she then wonders why nobody tells her anything. Sometimes she decides to add imaginations to her list of strange accomplishments, telling herself that "certain people" must not like her anymore.

The Problem

"It's a dysfunction, Lucy, and it starts with you." How often I have prayed and said, "What am I doing wrong Father?" I have literally lost track of how many times I've prayed that.

The reason I can identify with Lucy, is I've had many years of looking at myself with God's help. He has shown me the things I know, and sometimes even uses secular knowledge to give me understanding of what He is talking to me about.

Lucy wants to know, and she wants to feel useful and productive, just as we all do. She has a heart to serve others, and really wants to be of help. I feel for her, and I do feel her pain. She dearly wants to help, but part of her motive is a little selfish.

We may all have a little Lucy in us, but that doesn't mean we have to stay that way.

Try to remember if someone no longer seems to want to share their problems with you, it may be that you've been so eager to share what you know versus helping them grow, they may have decided to seek counsel elsewhere.

Lucy doesn't know how to listen, She only knows how to spout off answers she has tucked neatly into her belt of supposed "truths." She fails to see that one truth does not fit all who have that that similar problem. She likes to play counsellor, forgetting that life is not just about her having the answers. Lucy is sometimes a little immature (as I have been) And has not yet learned to quench her enthusiasm for knowing the answers to stop, think, pray and answer when the spirit of God leads her to do so.

In her heart, Lucy doesn't think she is harming anyone, but the truth is that bad advice only adds to the problem, and sometimes a person in trouble who gets bad advice can be driven to the breaking point, if we are not careful.

We all have areas we need to grow, but not all people will admit they need to grow. I believe we should keep a stance of learning and growing until the day we die. If we have lost that ability, we have lost any hope of having better relationships in the future, either with ourselves or with others. I also believe in urging others to grow.

If we continually call everything a sin OR just overlook it and do not talk about growing, how will it ever get done?

I found out I was like Lucy the hard way. How? I had a few faithful friends and loved ones tell me off for my unsolicited, untimely and un-helpful advice. One day a minister also said this to me, *"In your heart you are a very big girl, but you do need to grow."*

Do you think Jesus only meant to grow in the scriptures printed in our bibles? If that were true, nobody would be inventing anything, there would be no cars, planes or indoor plumbing. Nobody would think, dream, learn or discover how to make our lives better if we limited ourselves to the words on the pages of our bibles. So then it is okay to think, right?

"…grow in the grace and knowledge of our Lord and Savior Jesus Christ. To Him *be* the glory both now and forever. Amen." 2 Peter 3:18, (NKJV).

4. SCARY HARRY

Scary Harry could be a friend, a parent, both parents, or even a spouse. He or she could be a boss or a co-worker. Chances are unless you ARE scary Harry, you have encountered him. Chances are if you are Harry, you have been taught by someone like him at some point in your life via a bad example, whether a parent or someone else.

Harry wants to intimidate, make you cow down, and takes great delight in getting others to submit to him. He loves power. He can be female also, but for the sake of simplicity I'm sticking to Harry, and my apologies to all the nice guys named "Harry" out there, but he had to have a name.

If you lived in an authoritarian household, one where the rule is, "My way or the highway," you've probably been set up not to know what to do about Harry.

My first encounter with Harry was as a child. He could be unreasonable, a bully by today's standards, and he never let you explain. Harry liked to catch you in the act, hit you in the back, and make you feel very small and ashamed of yourself.

The boss I described in bossy bosses was also this "Scary Harry" type. I've seen him bully my children and bully me as well. He has temper tantrums and unpredictable fits of rage over what seems like nothing.

Sometimes he just glares at you but won't tell you why. He refuses to acknowledge people when they walk into a room, until later, when he decides you have done something out of line according to his strict and rigid standards.

Harry will say, "Why did you just do that?" In a policeman-like voice. You are thinking, "What, what did I do?" You don't know; and Harry likes it that way.

For those who are willing to learn and teachable and for those who truly want to better themselves, Harry is a very real monster to contend with. He doesn't show mercy and he doesn't cut anyone any slack.

I don't know exactly what makes Harry tick, but I do know his mannerisms become predictable after a time. Some will run from him, while others will spend their lives trying to please this man. Trust me, He cannot be pleased. His goal is to make everyone around him feel very small, so he can feel a bit taller.

He has trained himself not to feel guilty about what he does. Chances are, every time Harry felt he might be doing wrong, he defended himself and told himself he was being strong and not weak or bold and not meek. He might cherish sayings such as, "Do to others before they do unto you," Or "Nice guys finish last."

You won't win with Harry, not unless you are meaner than he is. If your aim is to not to be mean and naughty, I suggest you learn to how to dodge him.

I've quit jobs over Harry. There have been movies made about him, mostly stories about abuse and victims finally escaping from him.

Harry is not about to change, not so long as he's got new victims to mess with. You can call it a mental illness, or narcissism, or anything you'd like. He is mean, and he likes how he feels when he has the power over others that he ultimately craves.

As a Christian you can pray for him, as a humanist, you can try to do nice things and melt the savage beast. I have encountered quite a few Harry's in my life, and none of them have ever changed without first admitting they have a problem.

Just recently, last night in fact, I watched a movie about one who got Jesus and realized the error of his ways. It can happen, but I wouldn't bet on being the one to change Scary Harry. He's the guy you don't want to fight with. Here are some more tips on what I've learned about handling life with Harry.

Dodge and Duck

You've got to dodge this type of person, and not try to be close to them. This has been my experience.

Choose soft answers to turn away his wrath and try not to argue with them because you won't win. If they are a parent and you must deal with this, chances are you are going to get hit occasionally by a stray ball of belligerence.

People who are forced to deal with Scary Harry's need more confidence, more love for themselves, and more understanding that you can't change them. The reason you can't is because people have free will. Not everyone wants to be a nice person, and the sooner we learn that, the better off we are. We can pray, but we cannot change them.

I used to be very idealistic and believed that deep down, all people wanted to be good. This was one of the areas I had where my belt of truth was not on tight enough.

Here is one passage that may help you identify Scary Harry.

"But know this, that in the last days perilous times will come: For men will be lovers of themselves, lovers of money, boasters, proud, blasphemers, disobedient to parents, unthankful, unholy, unloving, unforgiving, slanderers, without self-control, brutal, despisers of good, traitors, headstrong, haughty, lovers of pleasure rather than lovers of God, having a form of godliness but denying its power. And from such people turn away!"

2 Timothy 3:1-5 (NKJV).

I see a lot of people out there who still possess this type of idealism; even when they have seen first-hand the carnage of a bully who has spun out of control.

Honey, I am so sorry; but sometimes we don't see until it punches us right in the eye. In the case of myself, I had to be abused by Harry for quite some time before I saw the light.

I want to share a few scriptures with you:

1. "A soft answer turns away wrath" Proverbs 15:1 (KJV).

2. "Let your moderation be known to all men" (Philippians 4:5 KJV).

3. "Dearly beloved avenge not yourselves...." (Romans 12:19 KJV).

King David ran from Saul and even hid from him for a time. (Book of 1 Samuel). Saul turned into a Scary Harry, and he stayed that way until the day he died.

David prayed for him, ran from him, and even blessed him with his words. He refused to obtain retribution, even when killing him would have been justified. I take great comfort in this old testament story because I see not only God's faithfulness to David, but also know that if God could not deliver Saul from himself because Saul did not wish to change, then it means he cannot change every bully I face either.

God could theoretically make someone change but he won't. Even the angels have free will, and some of them use that power of choice to rebel against God. God can woo them, send people to talk to them, and by his Spirit, even convict them. We must remember that in our bible there are cases of men who never do repent, sad as it is to hear. In our willingness to turn the other cheek may we also remember we are the temple where God dwells.

You might forgive someone for scuffing up the church or even breaking a window but would certainly not stand by and allow someone to tear it down without assertively fighting back. Why would we do less for ourselves, God's temple? It's too easy to fall into extremes. In my Christian walk, I've often gone from extreme mercy and martyrdom and have also fallen into a hyper-vigilance about not being abused. Neither is right, and those of us who have been abused must realize we need healing to be normal, and not become dysfunctional ourselves.

5. KNOW-IT-ALL-NELLIE

Know-it-all-Nellie always shows up when there are questions to be answered. She pretty much believes she knows everything, or at least a little something about every subject we've encountered. She's a little bit like Lofty Lucy, only she has more experience, and is harder to detour from her mission because she's positively sure she is right.

Unlike Lofty Lucy, Nellie has more facts on her side. She's studied the ins and outs of many topics and lights up anytime someone is needing some help or guidance with most anything. It's fine she wants to help, but a lot of times it becomes obvious after a time, that she can't seem to swallow statements such as, "Let me pray about it."

Pray about it? That is simply unacceptable to Nellie. Why? Because she already knows the answer, that's why. Nellie doesn't see the point in praying about something that God has quite clearly given her the brains to figure out. She has pride, a bit of knowledge on the puffy side, and she is not going to sit and let someone pray about something she already knows how to solve.

She may not mean to be, but Nellie is one of the biggest obstacles to people growing up in God. The other obstacle of course, is people not believing they need to grow.

What's in it for Nellie?

Nellie gets to feel important if she has the answer. It's almost a god-like rush for her to swoop in and save the day.

The trouble is, I was always a bit too goofy to come across as one who knows all the answers, otherwise, I might have tried it!

By now it probably sounds like I'm just throwing all these poor souls under the bus, and I'm not even done yet.

One clue in knowing you might be dealing with a Nellie, is the attitude you get when you dare to say no to her. Most that I have met of this type, have a great deal of pride, and do not respond well to feeling rejected.

Sometimes Nellie has the answers, sometimes she doesn't.

She'd like to shape and mold someone, which is God's job by the way, and have the person come out just perfect so she can take all the credit. It's rather like a living soul-version of playing with dolls. I had a friend once who wanted to dress me, fix my hair just right, and present me to the world "a new woman."

While I understood the vision and the goal, I also knew if I was re-vamped on the outside and not changed on the inside, God himself would not even be impressed. I would be spending the rest of my life trying to look good, while simultaneously trying to hide the fact my soul was messed up, all the time.

See my friends? I can see through these people because

I've been a little bit of all of them. I'm not here to try to make myself look important. My aim is to help you see a little of yourself in the mirror, or perhaps even understand your friends and loved ones a bit better. We also need to understand that everything is not "the devil."

Although he is behind the idea of people not growing and developing, his seeds of lies may have been planted so very long ago that his victims do not realize they've been duped. That's the reason praying for God to teach us by his Spirit, is so very important. He has a plan, tailor-made, just for you.

If a person is grown-up, sees the light about themselves, and God has revealed all truth about themselves to them, then the devil won't have a way in, any longer.

The devil also cannot upset a person who is standing in the full stature that God intended. He can't get to them, get them to react, or lead them astray. So, guess what? When someone upsets me, I may be upset for a time, but you can bet I will get with Jesus and start examining my own soul.

Nellie goes awry

There was a Christian company that offered to help with my first book. They said they were in business to help others with their knowledge, and I believe they meant well in the beginning. At some point I believe they had money problems and some things got out of hand with their business. Because of pride, they did not own up to it, and as a result, I was very angry with them for a long time. It was hard for me to forgive them.

The anger that Jesus was talking about (being angry with your brother) That puts us in danger of hell, is the kind that begins to take us away from the goal of who we are becoming in Him.

It's not so much we need to tolerate evil, as we need to realize what we can change, and what we cannot change. Do people sometimes rob us of a blessing? Yes, they do. I had an experience like this with a publishing company.

I was so angry with the company, I could hardly stop obsessing over how to solve it. Speaking of know-it-all Nellie, they claimed they would make my book better, market it better, and launch me if I had anything good to say. They claimed they had read my book and had chosen it from a great number of wonderful publications.

In the end, this all turned out to be a farce. Their purpose was to make money off me, and everyone else who submitted their book. The company said they were charging me a retaining fee, that would be reimbursed when the books started selling. They had experts on the phone, telling me what I needed to edit from my book, some of which was very important to the content. As they strained out some of the good stuff, I also learned they some actual errors in grammar, but it was too late.

I was furious with this company for a time, and furious with myself for trusting them. I must say I was little out of sorts with God too, wondering why he didn't let me know this would happen. Looking back now, I do believe they knew how to publish and truly did believe they were helping others with this company. The truth is however, I was at fault for letting my book go to them, and not staying surrendered to the Lord as my guide.

What is my point? Perhaps Nellie really wants to save people from a fate she endured. Perhaps she missed golden opportunities because of lack of a great outfit, or a great hair-do. I think this company meant to help and I had to forgive them.

I have no doubt in my mind that many of the people I will describe in this book have GOOD HEARTS. Not all, but most do have great intentions. They are not monsters, but they do need to realize that their perspective is not the only perspective.

If we get mad at other Christians and hide or run from them, spending all our time beating off devils in the spirit realm while simultaneously beating them over the head with the bible, or even cut them out of our lives one by one, how are we ever going to have those relationships we say are so important?

People may frustrate us, and they may not always seem to care they are causing us such great distress. I believe a combination of prayer, acquiring some knowledge, hearing from God, along with a willingness to communicate and hang in there is the answer.

The reason I say Nellie is often the greatest obstacle to growing in Christ, is because she is so busy coming up with answers for you, that you may not have a chance to learn from God.

If we don't learn from God, it's not as real to us, and doesn't seem to stick very well. If God's word in our lives is all because of second-hand information learned from other preachers, I it will not be enough for us to stand our ground when we are all alone in our trials. We need to know God for ourselves. It is crucial to not falling in sinking sand.

We cannot rely on Nellie. We need to trust God, himself.

6. SOME SOLUTIONS BEFORE WE MOVE ON

1. Do a self-check for hypocrisy

I think I've adequately covered the solution for us, which is to admit we need to grow and develop and become more Christ-like. It's just too easy to fall into the trap of saved by grace, and don't-need-to-change because God loves me just as I am.

He does love us as we are, but when a child does not develop in the natural, they call this developmentally disabled. Often a check is issued by the government for this condition, and there is no hope for anything to get better. Thank God that by his grace we can change, and we don't have to stay the way we are.

2. Decide not to judge

When I say don't judge, I mean to not slam the gavel and say in your heart; "There is no hope for them, they are too far gone." Judgement that condemns a person to no hope for any redemption, is far different than the type of judging we are doing here.

We must be as jurors and assess the situations around us, and realize there is sin, dysfunctional people, wounded people, unsaved people, and all kinds of people. There are even narcissistic people, which the hardest of all to deal with.

3. Accept, Forgive & Pray

I have found this to be a battle and a growing process, all at the same time Without quoting about ten scriptures, I want to say that accepting others as they are, and not how we want them to be, plus forgiving them for upsetting our apple carts and how they seem to ruin our days, and all the other messes that come with dealing with their dysfunctions, is more like a mountain than a mole-hill.

What we want to do is either clobber some over the head or avoid them. If my dysfunctional way meets up with your dysfunctional way, chances are there is going to be a very big problem. An example would be you were raised in a dirty house or you always saw your dad drinking and coming home late. Your mom would cry all the time, and you wondered why he would just not stop drinking.

When faced with a child who is now developing a drinking problem, all the bad feelings and memories come flooding back. Before you know it, you find yourself railing on this child, because there is no way you are going to see him/her grow up to be like your dad and the problems that went with it. It's these types of scenarios that make people say things like, "No, I cannot accept this."

If the fear level rises and their emotions are shaken, some people do wind up spiritualizing their responses and start banging their dysfunctional victim over the head with scripture, all the while acting dysfunctional themselves.

This is the reason why we must accept each person where they are, forgive them for shaking us up and wrecking our day, and pray for the solution. Every case is different, no two people are quite the same.

4. Ask God for Help

"If any of you lacks wisdom, let him ask God......."
(James 1:5 NKJV). I have asked God for wisdom thousands
of times. When he said he will give it to all without partiality, I
believe him. I know he doesn't expect us to flounder around
on this earth unequipped, and unable to attain how to handle
situations we encounter. We do have to give up our carnal
earthly ways however, *if we expect to possess his wisdom.
We also may have to give up on some people approving of
us* if they are not handling it the same way they would.

Asking for God's help may seem simple to us, but the
complication lies in the fact that what he tells you or leads
you to do may not line up with what everyone else is doing
or has been doing.

Remember my friends, this is one reason Jesus called his
way a narrow path. It's not obviously marked out for you and
everyone else may not be going that way.

I have found when I ask him, the answer he leads me to
varies from one person to the other. Do you like to be treated
like you have no face and no unique situation? Do blanket
answers always work for you? It's good to remember those
pat answers did not always work for us and take the extra
time to pray for God's answers. Take time to pray.

5. Carry on

After we have taken these steps, which may be after we
screamed, yelled and said out loud, "Why does this always
happen to me?" We need to just lay it down and carry on.
Worry really is like a rocking chair, and while I've spent many
hours of my life rocking back and forth wondering what to do
about something after I've prayed, I found it really gets me

nowhere. What works for me, is to wait for my opportunity to act on the solution God will show me.

There have been times I had no idea what to say or do about a person, and suddenly I watch for it and have this chance to speak and address the problem.

It's amazing that when we let go of something and pray, God never forgets what we have asked of him. In the world we are taught to shut people out and do tough love on addicts, then send co-dependents to weekly meetings.

If that works for you great, but what about the rest of the people who have issues to solve?

I know you know there are many people out there who need what I would call "Holy Spirit counselling" On many subjects. Can't God us you? Do you really need to give them a book or video? That's what we usually do, because many of us have no faith we ever have the right words to say.

What if we all believed we are ministers of the gospel, not only to get people to Jesus, but to cope with life's daily problems?

Can you imagine how much better things would be, if we all just believed we could?

The Vision to work out our Salvation

One of the biggest challenges for Christians, I believe, is to realize they have some brethren that are refusing to grow up, into the head, which is Christ. (Ephesians).

We suppose this will be automatic, not realizing that the word of God covers everything from being transformed by the renewing of our minds, to staying humble, to instructions on what the goal is. We need to become Christ-like.

You would not believe how many people argue with me and say things like; "We are not Jesus, and never can be." I never said I was Jesus, but I do want to be Christ-like.

The whole earth is groaning, waiting for the sons of God to manifest, but we need to grow up and become his sons (and daughters) after the example of the first-born son, which is Jesus Christ.

If you thought someone getting a new heart, liver transplant, or other body parts put in place to save their lives, that's nothing compared to the total transformation God wants to do in our souls.

When you become born-again, you have a spirit man that is perfect, which is why (1 John NKJV) God says you cannot sin. He is talking about your new born, newly-created spirit man that lives inside you.

That Spirit man still has a free will and must choose to rise and overcome the flesh, the soul, and everything else that is not renewed by the Spirit of God yet.

You and God together are in partnership strive to overcome all the areas of the flesh and soul that are not like him. This process is called overcoming, and it's important until the day we die.

Once we get to heaven of course, all things that are of the flesh will completely pass- away, and all things will become new. The life we live on this earth will only be victorious so long as we let his kingdom come (in us), his will be done (in us), On earth (in us), as it is in heaven. See? We get transformed by the Spirit of God and then things around us begin to change and conform to the power of his will.

I'd love to give you an easy solution about others, but the truth is, Lucy and the others must decide for themselves if they wish to grow or not grow.

I don't know if you've ever seen a stubborn child before, but many are so stubborn even with a good spanking they will still buck up against discipline, cross their arms and almost fight you to the death.

There are some like this among God's children. These have given their lives to Jesus, but like the Children of Israel, they are just plain stubborn at times.

I cannot honestly say that I am positive about this, but I believe these are the ones that wind up having to go through the consequences of their ways and God is sometimes silent with them until they realize at some point in their suffering, they did not ask to do things his way. Just a thought.

"And you have forgotten the exhortation which speaks to you as to sons: "My son, do not despise the chastening of the Lord, nor be discouraged when you are rebuked by Him;" Hebrews 12:5 (NKJV).

7 SKITTISH STEVIE AND SPIRITUAL STELLA

Steve is skittish because he's afraid. He's afraid of being deceived and he's afraid of getting things wrong and finding out later he was led to be a fool.

Whenever Steve is faced with a new concept or idea, He tends to just nod or say, "That's something to think about," and never gets back to the idea again. That's because he's afraid of it, but He doesn't want to say so.

I recall this time while I was visiting with a pastor's wife, she expressed to me how she feared some of the spiritual giftings.

"How do you know it's God, and not the devil?" She asked. Good question! Have we not see people act super-strange when they claimed it was God's Spirit? Yes, we have.

I have seen people enjoy a football game and jump out of their seats cheering on their team; but I also have seen some who lost their minds, and nearly started a riot, over losing a game. I don't stop going to football (or any other place) because people have acted weird about it. I do not stop pursuing all God has for me, just because there have been a few nut cases out there.

Stevie is skittish about anything that makes him uncomfortable, or anything he does not have understanding about. Here is the key, we can pray for understanding, we can encourage Steve to ask God what he thinks about a matter and then, we can give him pointers on what we have learned about the subject. That is called ministry, and we can do this too! We can encourage him, not to be so skittish.

Pentecostals are a little bit famous for being like Super-Spiritual-Stella. When Stella and Steve get together, it's not likely to be smooth sailing for either of them.

Yes, of course, tell people about the spiritual gifts Stella, but only as the Spirit leads you to do so. Are you aware Stella, how very immature you look, sometimes? You have not considered the passage that says if we teach a man about meat when he is content with vegetables, you are making him stumble, and therefore not walking in love.

Romans 14:2 (NKJV) refers to the eating of spiritual food, and how some do not believe something is okay for them. We need to grow (up) to learn and discern when is the right time to talk to someone about these spiritual giftings.

Stella is concerned Steve is missing out, and Steve is concerned someone will teach him deceptive things. What is the answer? The answer is, be gentle with Steve.

As I always say, Growing is the answer for both parties. If Steve is a disciple and truly follows Jesus, wanting to learn of him, Jesus will make sure he learns all he needs to know to fulfill his calling on planet earth.

If Stella applies her heart to learn from Jesus, he will also teach her not to be so overly righteous about gifts that came to her by his Grace. (Ecclesiastes 7:16).

We do not have to win the argument, put Steve in a choke-hold, or try to batter him into believing spiritual things. Steve is skittish, but he will get it if we just let him know we are not out to scare him or deliberately make things too weird for him.

Stevie's personality makes me think about why it's so important that everything is done in a spirit of gentleness. Some of Steve's reservations have to do with seeing those who have literally clashed the cymbals into his ears, spiritually speaking. All he heard was a very loud noise, and it frightened him.

Haven't we all been skittish at times? Unsure about the path that is before us? I think so. Let's not be too hard Steve. He just needs a little love, (and coaxing) to see that what is going is on is not all that scary, after all.

A Prayer: "Father please help us to truly see that we all need to grow (in Grace) and the knowledge of you. None of us have arrived and none of us has all the answers, but in you, we eventually can and will have all the things we are hungry for. Blessed are those who hunger and thirst Father, as Jesus said in Matthew 5. Please help us to continue to want more of you and less of our own ways. This is your very heart for us and help us to see it before it's too late. In Jesus' name we pray, Amen"

8 SMUG SALLY AND SCAREDY-CAT CLARA

Sally is smug, and Clara is scared. An interaction between the two might go something like this.

"Do you want to go up to the cities and see the races this weekend? Sally inquires.

Clara says, "No, it scares me all those people driving drunk, you know an accident seems to happen about every weekend up there, in the summer."

"Oh poo," says Sally, I've been there thirty times or more and nothing ever happens to me. Besides, if you are meant to die in an accident, there isn't much you can do about it."

Clara may be an introvert or has a long history with failure in social interactions. It could be she was teased in school, tried to make friends and failed, or her family life included a whole lot of belittling. We don't know.

I had unreasonable fears for years, after I was the victim of a violent crime. I didn't know how to explain to people that dark places at night, in neighborhoods I was not familiar with, nearly put me into a panic at times. If Smug Sally is a Christian, she is more likely to say something like, "Perfect love casts out fear, so I will pray for you not to be so scared all the time."

Comments like this while they are true, can feel like salt on a wound because Clara doesn't wish to be scared all the time. For her, it's not even a conscious decision. If she had been traumatized or abused or like me, or a victim of a violent crime, she needs to make peace with why it happened before she can even begin addressing the fear.

I remember journaling and trying to make peace with why the violent crime happened. Part of the time I blamed myself, part of the time I blamed the perpetrator.

Why had I opened the door? I remembered a little nudge down inside telling me not to. Why Had I not listened to it? Why were such violent people out there anyway? And why did he pick me? Did God allow this? Was I being punished for not answering the call on my life in the first place? These are questions I had. For a long time, I thought God allowed it as a type of discipline, but I realize now that wasn't the case.

I was hurt because I was not tuned in to the idea of listening to God's Spirit. While he may lead us to die for him once we've counted the cost, He does not lead us into places to be abused by the devil or his clan. Even Jesus ducked and dodged the Pharisees until his mission on earth was over and it was time for him to die for a specific reason. More on this another time, as we are talking about Clara and Sally right now.

Clara could have had an experience as a child at a race such as the one Sally is inviting her to, and it went bad for her. People tend to shove traumatic events to the back of their minds, having no idea when the bad memory may affect them.

It's not a conscious thing, and it's certainly not a spiritual thing. It has to do with their mind. Their heart doesn't want to be scared, but their mind is saying they must be. The answer may be spiritual, but the person may need to feel accepted or loved before they can receive the seed of God's word into their heart.

Smug Sally wants to help; All she can see is the need for Clara to get out and do things without fear. Clara is perhaps hoping to establish a relationship where she can finally talk about the things that have always troubled her. There is a conflict, and it's under the surface, where it cannot be seen with the natural eye.

This struggle is in the heart, which needs to be prepared like soil needs to be ready to receive a good seed. Religious dogma does not help us see this, but Jesus will.

One day, if Sally doesn't stop pushing, Clara may just run from the relationship. Sally smug if she is true to her choice of paths may just tell herself, "I tried to be her friend, but I guess it wasn't meant to be."

After losing some good relationships, giving up on too many, and running into some of the same problems numerous times, I began to pray more and more for understanding of the turbulence that goes on amongst people.

I so desperately wanted to understand and lend a helping hand to see relationships grow and flourish. It's so easy for some, to just fall into the trap of blaming the devil for everything, or assuming someone just wants to "be in the dark" as we so smugly call it. Not everyone who disagrees with us is in the dark. Not everyone who won't listen to the scripture we just quoted is rebellious. We need to figure out

45

if we are smug Sally (or have some of her traits) and get over ourselves if we truly want to make a difference.

I have been a scaredy-cat and have met many

Who does want fear? Not me. It's like a prison, and it prevents us from doing all that we desire to do.

I'm afraid of driving in fog, and of wasps and bees.

I have overcome the fear to some degree, but there are certain things that truly freeze me up sometimes. I am aware that if I fear things, I may cease to live my life as abundantly as I'd like to.

I've met a lot of smug Sally's who insisted there was nothing to fear, and yet had fears of their own they did not even recognize. This is called hypocrisy. It's difficult to receive from such a person, don't you think?

Some have a literal fear of anyone seeing their house messy, while another person fears ever being seen without her hair being perfectly done. If we are immature, we so easily see the faults of others, and not ourselves.

I don't see any reason we have to be abrasive or mean over our religion. Scaredy-Cat Clara has so many traits I can relate to. She doesn't want to mess things up. Some fearful people are afraid to discipline their children, fearing they will do it wrong and hurt them for life. Others have so much fear their child will mess up, they go overboard with the discipline and cause harm in a different way.

Smug Sally (who needs to get humble), always has an answer for every situation, a lot like Lofty Lucy, and Know-it-all-Nellie. The difference is, she is smug that what she does works for her and believes it should work for you also.

Here's a scripture for you to ponder:

When a man's ways please the Lord, He makes even his **enemies** to be **at peace** with him." Proverbs 16:7 (NKJV)

Realizing God wants me to be at peace with people If I can be, also helps me to have direction in not just jumping to conclusions or walking away from people the minute they seem to conflict with my beliefs or even my current understanding of God's word.

You see, it doesn't always mean a spirit of fear is coming on this person if they have fears. They may need to understand that fear is hindering them, but they also need a little space to figure out why this is happening. One of the truths that revolutionized my prayer life was the fact that I got hurt by smug Sally's prayers.

Why is this, you wonder? It's because there is freedom in knowing the truth about what really happened. This bible truth which declares, "The truth will make you free," really is a powerful thing. I was hurt by Sally, and the hurt led to fear of listening to anyone who reminded me of her or anyone who acted like her. When I do that, have limited who God can work through and who he cannot, all because I've been hurt and have developed fear.

After I forgave these incidents and asked God to keep me following him and trusting in him, I can trust God to work through Sally again, despite her human issues.

Do you see? The truth really can make us free. We now know what's going on, and can decipher when Sally is smug, or when Clara is just scared.

We do not any longer, feel we must throw these babies out with the bathwater, or write them off as not being capable of ministering to others in the Lord just to protect ourselves.

Even babies have their spiritually sound moments. Am I right? God uses children, too!

The walls are coming down, aren't they? Can you hear the noise of your self-protective walls just falling? Me too.

Prayer:

"My belief system should always be subject to adjustments, according to your plan, Father.

Help me to stay surrendered to you. Help me to learn from you, and to grow. In Jesus' name, Amen "

9 LECHEROUS LARRY & OTHER PREDATORS

A story of sexual abuse

There are wicked people and there are dysfunctional people. People who have not arrived at the full stature that God intended but are trying to get there and have a great heart, are certainly different from a person lost in a world of sexual perversion and sexually violent ways.

We must know the difference, for if we don't, we will fail to protect those God intended for us to protect and defend.

I lived this first-hand. It was closer to my door than I ever wanted to think. Someone very close to me was abused sexually, and it was the single most horrible moment of my life when I found out about it.

Without going into too much detail, I will just say it was heart-wrenching and produced incredible anger, rage and hostility toward the perpetrator that was beyond reason. I am sorry to say that many do not realize until something like this happens to them (or someone they love), It's kind of theoretical to them. Until you have seen the trail of debris left behind by someone shattered by rape or sexual abuse, we simply have no clue what all goes on with such events.

In my experience, sexual abuse to a child, rape, molestation, all these types of things tend to cause unreasonable fears and anxiety, mistrust toward others, and a multitude of other symptoms. Many books have been written by psychologists, most of which suggest we need therapy for the rest of our lives, or at the very least; medications and therapy to cure the side-effects of these atrocities.

Christian books often tend to have some formatted plan that is supposed to work, but there really is no "one-size-fits-all" answer to the healing and restoration that is needed for people who have suffered any type of sexual abuse.

Sex is personal and intimate. It doesn't matter if the abuser sees it that way, it's still very personal, and most women who have been molested or raped feel ashamed, defiled, unworthy, and a host of other symptoms which arise. Some spend the rest of their lives angry, and some will never trust men. There is no way to cover all the symptoms in one book. As far as I'm concerned, the answer that is the most likely to succeed, is God and his council.

If you think about it for a minute, God came up with sex, made us, and he designed humans in the first place. It stands to reason he has the best plan as to how to repair us, when we are broken.

My apologies Larry, I don't mean to pick on you, and I know you come in many forms, some are even female. Your name could be Mike, Joe, or even Ned.

Chances are, you became lecherous because someone taught you sex is all there is. It could be you were taught to disrespect women or see them as objects. You may have also had a dad who taught you to be this way; and have no idea your ways are loathsome to women. I feel for you, but I cannot tolerate your ways.

When I was fifteen, I got a job at an ice plant. There was a guy there who was about 50 years older than me, who made a pass at me one day when we were alone in the office. He planted his lips on me. I was both horrified and afraid, and quit the job directly after that. He chased me down, offered me payment for sex, and drove me further from having any understanding of it all, along with much residual fear.

When I was in the military, I had numerous guys make passes at me, and I heard many men make comments and talk about women like they were objects. Lecherous or sex-driven men show up everywhere, and although things are changing, in my generation most did not know what to do about them.

They lurk in the hallways waiting for a chance to pounce on someone with their unwanted advances. They behave like animals whenever they get the chance; and they often are married. What do we do about these guys?

So often in my experience, those of us who want nothing to do with them; dodge them. Is it a spirit, or is it a condition?

How Church people handled it

"They have a perverse spirit," I heard one say, "We need to pray they get delivered from it." When I was a young Christian and was trusting God to work through the elders and leaders of the church, I went right along with this ideal.

Years later, my prayer target was still hooked on porn and doing all kinds of unmentionable things. He had been abused, he had witnessed his own sister being raped.

Psychology would say he was a victim who now needed understanding and help to understand himself and what is making him tick. Much of Christianity implied we just needed to have faith and pray harder, because the devil and the problem will then have to go if we only have enough faith and patience.

If the person who is living in a perverse sexual lie enjoys the lie, sees no problem with the lie, and truly believes they aren't hurting anyone (or perhaps doesn't care) there is not going to be any happy ending to this story, for us or for them.

How do I know? I lived it.

I am begging you, please Christians, do not think you can pray away every evil trait someone has. Spend some time praying you have wisdom or truth, and perhaps you can assist others to escape their living hell rather than focusing on your prayers on changing someone who has zero desire to change. It was hard for me to learn this, but God used the example of my own children to show me how he feels about us as his people. He wants the devil outside of our realm and not tormenting us all the time. This means that as God's people, we must learn to help others escape their torment, and not just spend all our time praying for the perpetrators.

I was raped, and my children suffered as victims of a sexual crime by a church member. The issue was treated so lightly by church people, I thought I might go insane om the struggle to heal, forgive, and get past it. I don't want your sympathy, because God got me through it. But my heart cries out for you to be aware of what can happen to a person when they are unprotected from such incidents by the church.

In the book of 1st Corinthians, (NIV) Paul suggested we turn over a person to the enemy and let them live with the demons they have invited. (1 Corinthians 5:5 NIV).

In the natural realm, there are laws against crimes and we must not be hesitant to let the laws of the land work in our favor. I got so busy with love-love-loving, I forgot that God loves me too. Jesus wants us to forgive, sometimes give people another chance; but our passion to save people from hell must not exceed our understanding that he wants us (his children) to have protection and abundant life.

It wasn't until something happened to my children, that I realized how God must have felt when it happened to me. It was then that I knew he did not just stand back and allow it, to discipline me. I would never do that to my children, and neither would he.

The zeal of the Lord is great, but if our example is to love the unlovable to the point we allow them to abuse us, then compare it with the apostles going to prison, or John being be-headed, we are not using God's wisdom.

Those people died specifically for the cause of Christ and the gospel. They did not suffer and die at the hands of random abusers who just wanted to abuse them. We need the whole gospel and the whole council of God. We need to understand that God is with us to make decisions that are not always about tolerance, and letting criminals get away with whatever they wish to do to us.

If the problem was a devil, Jesus cast it out. In the case of a man who was sinning so blatantly in 1 Corinthians they "turned him over' to the evil one so that he might be saved. This meant he was going to suffer what he was alone and suffer the consequences of his own decisions, rather than just freely spreading his evil ways to others. Sexual sin defiles the church and the body of Christ and should not be tolerated.

If you're been abused

If you have been abused or feel the need to keep taking abuse in the arena of sex, I do encourage you to get with God if you are a Christian and ask him to take you all the way down to the roots of why it's been happening. I have kept journals for years. God and I have worked through many issues I had, including a lack of understanding about the role of women and sexuality. This is an area that would require another book to address it all but suffice to say if you are a victim of someone's dysfunctional ways; chances are you have some of your own that is allowing this to happen.

There is an old saying, "People treat you exactly how you let them." If you are allowing abuse, you probably need to look at some dysfunctional areas of your own. I have had to do this; and I will address it during the last part of this book.

We live in a time when we know that Lecherous Larry and his friends are not supposed to be abusing us in the work place. The difficulty for Christians is that when it's their spouse, their uncle, their dad, or whoever else in the family doing the perpetrating. Often these will go to the church, but the church often does not preach about these subjects, and as a result, very few have any sort of support group to help people deal with such thing incidents.

I want to say it can be a long hard road to healing, and to recovery, from these matters. You don't need a psychologist necessarily, although I do recommend arming yourself with some knowledge about these treacherous types.

If you have dealt with these things and more, you are not alone. I have suffered it, I have had friends who suffered it, and we've talked about it in hushed tones around some coffee and pie. God is with you. He wants to counsel you, and he can be your healer, as well.

I want to assure you; God wants to lead and guide you through these things. He's your good Father. Claim him as your own. He has already claimed you a long time ago at the cross.

I leave you with a partial description from the book of Isaiah about Jesus may it bless your heart.

"And His name will be called Wonderful, Counselor, Mighty God, Everlasting Father, Prince of Peace." Isaiah 9:6 (NKJV).

10 DRAMA QUEENS AND ALL-ABOUT-ME PEOPLE

They seem to have to be the center of attention, and they are good at it. This is the reason we call them queens. I've heard men be called drama queens also. It seems we all have some pre-conceived notion it's a womanly trait. Do you think this is true?

These types of people capture you, and make sure you cannot ignore them. They are the types that often blow things out of proportion, or often take center stage with their story, no matter what story you were telling first.

Drama Queens come in all shapes and sizes. Some are part-time while others seem to be at it full-time in their dramatic endeavors.

It may surprise you, that some of the antics I put in this chapter falls under the title of Drama Queens may not be what you first anticipated. Here are three types I know of.

1. Prayer Drama
2. Fellowship Drama
3. Work Drama
4. Family time Drama
5. Friendship Drama

Examples:

I am in a café with others, and we are having a discussion among ourselves.

Queenie walks in, sits down at the table, and begins to tell us what is going on with her and her life right now, seemingly oblivious to the idea anyone was having a conversation before she arrived. We all wait patiently for her to get done talking, and try to re-capture the conversation that was going on before she walked in.

When this pattern of behavior continues, there comes a time when we see her anywhere near our gathering place, we find ourselves wanting to find a new or different gathering place, just to avoid Queenie. We know if this person is near us, she will always barge in with this ridiculous and interruptive behavior.

I am working on a project, and tell D.Q. (short for Drama Queen), that I have much to do today. I take five minutes to brief her on what I need to do, and why it's so important.

She or he seems to completely forget what I said, and barges in on my project time later that day, certain that what they need is more important than what I am doing right now. They are not bleeding, they are not in a crisis, but just want to know where something is located, or have some other question that is so urgent to them right now, they are positive it's far more important than whatever I was doing.

I am upset, of course, having spent time explaining my impending duties, earlier in the day.

Drama queen gets even more dramatic at this point and says, "Fine, I will just stay away from you then," and storms off in a big huff, leaving a trail of guilt behind her/him.

Drama queen at prayer time will interrupt and say, "We need to pray about_____" and is convinced this prayer, (whatever is on their mind), is more important than your prayer

. Full of self-importance and having trained themselves not to be ignored by anyone, they will even quench a move of God's spirit and not seem to be aware of it.

There is a force in her voice that demands to be listened to. She is bold as brass and tough as iron. You don't' ignore drama queens, they are forces to be reckoned with.

When I was a DQ

Before I move on with this topic, I will share that I was once left out of a very important occasion with my family, due to the fact they felt I was a drama queen.

The exact words were this: "I didn't invite you because I didn't want drama." Wow. That hurt me, but it also made me think, as well as examine myself.

As I reflect on some of my history with this person, I could indeed see where they would think that about me It was certainly not an easy pill to swallow; but I did adjust, as a result, prayed for me to do better!

Remember, I am not writing this book because I know everything. I would never presume to think this way. I am writing what I have experienced, hoping that you will see with me; that there are personality types and people who are in different stages of growth and development.

Not everything is a demon and not everything is a pre-meditated sin. Some stuff we experience is just the endless possible quirks humans are prone to have.

I think in the Christian realm of church and gatherings, we get so used to praying about everything we don't just say things like, "Look, I was just talking that was kind of rude.'

Can we take someone aside and say something to them? Or is that too scary? And if too scary, Why?

Drama queens that are dramatic about God, often get chosen to be leaders in the church realm. I once met a woman who was very dramatic and yet, seemed very on fire for God at the time. She was asked to sing and lead music before anyone got to know her.

One day I was walking up to the door of her place of business, and heard dishes breaking and her husband and her screaming at one another. The fight went on and on, and later their restaurant and their home became closed up and abandoned.

People like drama queen at times, because they are not boring. This woman was always colorful and fun to be around, until the fun time was over with and we all wished she could settle down and behave herself.

Much like the class clown in school who never stopped having to be the center of attention, drama people can be over-the-top and even ridiculous; but never seem to realize the effect they have on other people.

I think drama queens could be asked a parable-style question, the way Jesus did when he spoke to the multitudes.

"Let me ask you," We might say to D.Q., "I was talking om a café and this person interrupted, and was very rude to me, what do you think I should do about it?"

D.Q. Just might know the answer. Just a thought.

You may be amazed to find that once you have forgiven a person, prayed for yourself, and then prayed for them as well, how easily the answers come to you.

The truth is however, we get so full of bible-knowledge as Christians, we sometimes forget to use our brains and even common-sense, in our interactions with other people.

"And just as you want men to do to you, you also do to them likewise" Luke 6:31 (NKJV).

11. Helpful Helen

Helpful Helen just called me. I was about to write a segment on this book and the phone rang. She had noticed I'd been helping a family member while they recover from surgery and found it necessary to tell me for the second time, that I should go to this certain organization, and find out if I could get paid for doing this service.

I was gracious, even though I had already thought about the possibility and decided against it for numerous good reasons. Helen was adamant as she said; "Well wouldn't it be nice to make money for doing that?" "Yes," I said, "But I don't think it would work in this situation because......" At this point, Helen jumped in, and stated that's what I should do, that's what she did, and I could really use the money.

I'm paraphrasing, but the fact remains, she was pretty determined to get me to see things her way. Did I ask her to borrow money? No, I did not. In the past when I had this sort of difficulty; it was usually because I asked for prayer at the church for about financial problems.

Helen has popped up a few times in my life. She always knows best, according to her, and her ideas are not to be discounted. She is an expert on every subject except the subject of relationships and how they should really work. In this recent conversation, I did try to graciously get around the unsolicited advice. I said; "I will consider what you've said, thank you."

She said; "Don't let me down on this one."

What? Don't let her down? What is that supposed to mean? I pondered it for a little bit, baffled that she would take it so personally if I did not heed her directive. We are not close friends, and she has no reason I can see to care if I did or did not take her advice. Does she need to be important? Does she think her advice was From God? I didn't ask her because I think I said something like this;

"Did you know a lot of people give me advice about what I should be doing?" I then added a quip that was basically asking if I look to be dysfunctional. She got a little put-off, and the conversation ended there. For now.

I have dealt with these types before. There was my mother-in-law, who would now laugh with me I'm sure (she is in heaven), but she used to get on me, about why I use red potatoes and not white, and how come I didn't talk to her when I first got up in the morning, and, would tell me what types of jobs I should look for. I loved her dearly. The difference was that in her case, she didn't obsess over it if I did not take her advice.

When someone gets focused on you, and what you ought

to be doing, and were not asked for advice I believe they have trespassed and crossed the line, as far as I'm concerned. Even God does not step in without an invitation. He may woo you to give him an invitation, but that's the reason why this world is so messed up; He does not jump into people's faces and say; "Look here, I'm God. I have the best advice in the universe and you had better be listening to it, or else."

Incidentally, this type of person will usually do this unsolicited advice thing until they finally hit a target. Like a hunter hitting the bird; they are encouraged; and go looking for someone else to bonk with their magic bullet. Most people avoid them, and what is a body to do? Do we tell them they are giving unsolicited advice all the time, and it's rude? And if we do; are we being just like them? If they didn't ask us; "Why do people avoid me, run from me, and hustle out of the room?" Then what can we really say?

It's no wonder in church; that the pastors often want to keep everyone busy with potlucks, scriptures, sing-alongs, and fairly monitored activities. It's behind closed doors or out of the church walls this stuff happens. Helen knows better than to talk over the pastor while he's preaching, or even go up to him and say things like, "Did you ever think about preaching something different next time?" No; she would not do that because then she would get caught.

See? People know better, and they really do. Deep down they know they are being kind of naughty, but they do it anyway because it feels good, or makes them feel important, or whatever the goal is in every case.

Lecherous Larry does it in the hallways when nobody is looking. Smug Sally pulls herself together when an authority figure walks in the room. Know-it-all-Nellie pretends to be humble and demure when anyone important is around. They know better, because they know deep down what grown-up behavior is, and what it isn't.

So much for me saying anything we don't already know, eh? We know things, but sometimes we need someone else to say it. We realize then, "Wow, I knew that."

That is what happens to me every time I read a truly great book or hear a great sermon. I think to myself, "Wow, that's so true." These are our light-bulb moments. I hope you are getting some here.

"Please Lord let it be, in Jesus' name, Amen"

Repeat after me:

"The Lord is my Shepherd. He guides me." He restores my soul. He leads me in the right paths. When someone speaks for him, it's in harmony with what I already know, deep down." (Psalm 23, NIV).

Did you know taking the advice of a Christian who is not completely renewed in the Word of God by growing up in him first, before they council you, could be a disaster?

Please be careful who you seek advice from. It's best to seek the Lord, first.

12. Preachy Petunia

Jesus didn't ask us to think about his word 24-hours a day. In fact, for those of us who get preachy, we may need to realize someone must be the trash man, someone must fix things, someone must do the laundry and dishes, cooking and cleaning, and making jam or jellies. To be good at this, they must think about what they are doing.

God's Spirit impressed on me once as my husband was doing a large project, that it took a lot of thinking for him to do what he was doing, and that he was anointed and blessed to that as a service to others. We can love the bible and talk about it, but it's wrong to believe we are superior somehow; just because we are talking about the bible.

The bible is a wonderful tool, resource, reminder and so many other things to help us live this life the way God intended. So many in the bible were craftsmen, wood-workers, tent-makers, and the like. I am embarrassed about how often I've been Preachy, just because that was my favorite topic. I sometimes excused myself from being selfish and not listening to others and what they had to say; and all because I thought my topic matter was superior to theirs somehow. Ouch.

I am, or have been, and still am at times, Preachy Petunia, so I can understand this one better than some other characters in this book. Being a preacher is not a bad thing, it's just any time we get out of balance, we look and see distorted to others, somehow. I think we need to all remember this and be more aware of what we're portraying to others. Don't you?

She's a little different from the others in that she loves the bible, wants to talk about it all the time, and doesn't necessarily have a motive to show off or just spout her knowledge.

Petunia just wants to make sure the atmosphere around her does not get inundated with carnal thinking, or maybe she is afraid just how far the gossip or sailor talk might go.

I know in my case, my goal to think about what is pure and lovely is often obscured with the negative, gossipy and even downright slanderous conversations

Before I go further, I want to share something my husband said to me about the upper room in the bible.

He said, "When they were up there tarrying for forty days, what did they talk about?" I was stumped. At first, I said, "They were tarrying!" He's referring to when they were waiting for the Holy Spirit to show up.

I said, "They probably prayed." He said, "24-hours a day?" Again, I was stumped.

"Did they maybe talk about their donkeys?" He said, "Or Maybe the best kind of donkeys?" "I don't know," I said, (all frustrated with him). His words stuck to me, as I thought about how God spoke to me once and told me I was in danger of alienating everyone around me. At that time, you could not get me to talk about anything but the bible. I'm quite sure and know that I frustrated a lot of people.

I wasn't trying to be bad, I was just gung-ho about Jesus, and determined to stay true, and keep my mind focused on him. If someone wanted to talk for an hour about food, babies, guns, mechanics, how to chlorinate a swimming pool, how to deal with changing a tire the right way, or any of that, it wasn't as important as keeping my mind on the words of God.

The bible was my favorite subject matter, but some self-righteousness crept in. As we all know, GOD is the most important subject, right? Therefore, I felt very justified by this behavior.

If He is the way, the truth, and the life, isn't truth important, also? And it doesn't always have to be the truths we find in our bibles, either. It can be every day stuff, Petunia, and I say this with lots of love, too.

What Petunia should do

As I said, there is nothing wrong with talking about the bible or preaching, at times. It can and does however, get to be ridiculous and extreme for some people. My husband had to say to me a few times, "You've been talking about this for an hour now." I would get going about the bible and get all on fire, animated, preaching, and would just go on and on.

Someone had to stop me. My husband was willing and did. When he first started, I cannot say I took it well, either.

Pentecostals are notorious for calling everything that is not the bible "worldly." TV is bad, games are bad, fun is bad. I had one lady who read my first book say to me, 'This is the only book I've ever read other than the bible." And she liked it by the way and could not put it down. This was my first book, Grace to the Rescue.

Petunia needs to ask God to help her grow and see things through his eyes. She is a little girl wearing big-kids' clothing. She was taught she has arrived, and just needs a little help seeing that God sees her as she will be (New Creation) but she has not arrived there yet. Petunia needs to grow, no matter how much scripture she's learned.

Petunia also may need to be prepared for someone to say to her; "So why do you only talk about the bible all the time, aren't there other subjects?"

She may get defensive, feel a bit persecuted and misunderstood, but in the end, Petunia will be okay. After all, she is studying a great subject, Right? And, she is trying to prove herself worthy, to Jesus.

Did you know, being overly-righteous can ruin you? I know, I wondered about that too, but it's true. You can read it in Ecclesiastes, chapter 7.

I am here to tell you, once I stopped preaching all the time and listened to others, I learned many new things.

I cannot speak for others, but here are some honest reasons I preached all the time. I hope this will help you see the possible motive behind this behavior.

1. I did not like to argue with others over opinions. Because I believe God's word to be full of undisputable truths, I would use it to stop arguments.

2. I wanted to bring people into the experience I was having and got overly zealous trying to persuade them to join me in following Jesus.

3. I was afraid of beliefs and things of this world getting into my mind or spirit, seeing it as a contaminate against God's holy word.

4. Preaching made me feel safe and kept me from having to answer the hard questions people often ask about God's word. I was not prepared to answer.

5. I was trying to prove myself qualified to talk about Jesus at all.

If we find ourselves preaching and starting a holy war of sorts, every time the atmosphere around us gets uncomfortable, we are not growing. We are like children slinging around the sword of God, in a frantic effort to keep our enemies at bay.

I can look back and laugh at my behavior now I times past, but the sad thing is, I see people that act like this all the time, and they alienate everyone around them. They are not winning anyone over to Christ in most cases, and have been labeled weird, quirky or even nuts by many. Is this the testimony Jesus is after? I do not think so.

For those of you who are not so preachy, you are probably thinking, "Yes, knock it off that preaching all the time,

"We'll get to you, my dysfunctional little pretty!"

"It is good to grasp the one and not let go of the other. Whoever fears God will avoid all extremes." Ecclesiastes 7:18 (NIV).

13. Picky Pete

Petunia, in my case, is married to this fellow. I love my husband very much, but he really is fussy about what he eats, where he sleeps, and so many other incidentals.

He must have a feather pillow, and it must go with us on our trips. His fussiness over food was almost our un-doing, a few times in our marriage.

Tim likes his potatoes with ranch dressing and it needs to be the kind you mix or it's no good to him. He prefers mayonnaise to salad dressing, beef over chicken, and soup is never a meal as far as he is concerned. He likes his eggs a certain way and real butter, not margarine. Most of these ways have rubbed off on me, and because I cook for him, I've become a bit fussy too.

Is it dysfunctional to have specific taste? I would say not, unless it becomes an obstacle to daily living. If you cannot afford what you like or refuse to socialize with someone because they happened to make chicken (and you are not allergic to chicken) I might have to say it's on the extreme side of thinking, and therefore, dysfunctional, according to God's holy standards of being like him.

Jesus made his disciples fish, and he gave the multitudes fish with bread. I'm pretty sure if they had ranted at him and said; "Where's the beef?" He might have given them that Jesus look. You know the one. Along with that, he might have said,

"Did you just question what I served you?" "Did I not tell you I was the son of God?"

The people of God in the Old Testament got in huge trouble one time, for complaining about food. If you don't know the story it's in the book of Exodus.

In Numbers 11:6 they complained; "We never see anything but this manna!" (Paraphrased).

I don't think preaching so much is a worse sin than being picky. Picky Pete is married to me, so I'm allowed to say,

"Wow, you are really picky." In Marriage we can do this, you know? As long as we love each other, pray together, and understand we are both accepted, but realize we need to keep growing, I think we'll be just fine.

For those who are not married, sometimes we don't go deep enough in the friendship to ever address such issues.

We don't have to live together, so why bother?

In marriage we are forced to deal with things. With friends, it's far too easy to let it go and keep it shallow.

I was protective of my Pete at one time, so I took a can of corned beef hash when I went visiting somewhere one time. The Hostess was shocked when I whipped out this can of hash and asked if I could cook it for him.

"I was going to make something else," she said, and I knew he wouldn't eat it. That my friends, was a hard day.

The best way to handle it, is to let Pete take his licks when others want to scold him about being picky. This way, he must address the problem, not you.

Picky Pete, Greedy Gertrude, Maggie the Gossip, and Con-Artist Phillip are other characters that come to mind right now. I do think we are starting to get the picture here, am I correct?

I think part of the reason the characters in this book are often found running around in church circles, is nobody knows what to do about it, or think it's not important.

It is important however, because it's the little things that add up into big things, over time.

Churches are full of messed-up people who came to Jesus, broken, hurting, and needing his love. We don't have to change everything in a day, but we can communicate to each other and not have fellowship feel like Chinese water-torture.

The problem is, we know how to deal with sin, chapter by chapter, verse by verse, but we often do not know how to deal with the mannerisms and habits of the dysfunctional, including ourselves. It's a topic we don't often talk about, or even take time to explore.

I had a friend once say to me, regarding this dysfunctional person she knew, "I can love her, but I do not like her." How sad. Furthermore, how often does this happen in church gatherings? Is this the reason we often have difficulty fellowshipping with one another?

Could this be the reason we get uncomfortable with any setting other than formatted bible studies, conferences, and settings where nobody hardly talks to each other?

When is it time to start dealing with some of these issues in a practical way? I wonder, should we start today?

14. All the others

Crazy Curt, Ruthless Ruth, Maggie the gossip. Okay, I'll use one on myself; How about, Lazy Laura? I used to be lazy, sometimes I relapse, and let the house work get behind. We have cons artists, spacey invaders, and people who forgot to bathe. There are judgmental people cynical people, and sarcastic people.

There are people who run to the front of the line at a potluck and take gigantic portions, leaving other to wonder if there will be any left when their turn comes.

We have people that steal from us but are not full-time thieves. Some steal out of desperation while others make it their passion. People commit sexual sins but are not leading a promiscuous lifestyle. In the church, we often want to label someone, so we can protect ourselves and our children from the illusion that, "sin is okay."

In our efforts to cleanse ourselves from associating with sinful people, we often become hypocrites in the process, and wonder why nobody wants to come to church.

Prideful Pattie, Self-Righteous Sam, and Intolerant Igor do not present Jesus accurately to a dying world.

If we use the bible as our only guide in it is word-for-word detail and not look beyond the words before us, seeing other unseemly traits we may have other than the ones prevailing in that time in history, we may fail to see ourselves in the mirror, as we really are. It took some common-sense people, along with the willingness to communicate with others, to help me see blasting everyone around me with the word of God every time I see a trait I don't like, without first growing up myself, is just plain rude.

The main point of this book is to annihilate the idea that any of us is perfect or has arrived. We say we know this, as we judge certain faults and dysfunctions relentlessly while conveniently overlooking our own inner-yard. The word dysfunction implies a person or object not functioning, the way it was intended to function.

What started out as a term used mostly on those who drink too much, use drugs, or act co-dependent. Gambling habits, criminal behavior and some dysfunctions lead to jail time. If every sin or dysfunctional way was a crime, we'd all be in jail by now.

The truth is.............

That nobody is right or wrong in any of these situations. They may need to grow, but they don't have to grow. You can't make them grow.

Preachy Petunia wants to find a scripture to point out the error of someone's ways. Sometimes we get in fear and try being Smug Sally or Know-it-all-Nellie. The worst thing is, if we keep going this way and refuse to grow at all (or see the error of our ways) we could become Bitter Bert, or Pharisee Freddie.

Too often in the church, I've heard, "

They are a Pharisee". Pharisees were the elitists and religious folks that Jesus dealt with in his time. Now let's face it; someone that has a bit of control problem, or someone that isn't getting the heart of Jesus right now; should not necessarily be labeled a Pharisee. My labels are far better. I am laughing as I say this, because I don't really believe that.

I'm just a girl trying to get across some truths we all need to realize, and one of them is we all have our issues. We really do not have room to judge in the sense of saying anyone is hopeless, even though we may want to, sometimes.

I believe God is okay with humor and talking about flowers, goats, sheep, pigs, cars, toilets, electricity and the list goes on. It's okay to think, and it's okay to work hard and think about what you are doing while you are doing it. We don't have to feel bad about our earthly knowledge, we just need to surrender all things to him.

I have realized for a long time now, we need to find ways to grow up together and still love each other while we are doing that. Picky Pete doesn't call all the shots, and neither does Control-Freak-Freida. The most grown-up person should make the decisions, and not the person who is the loudest or having the biggest tantrum.

We need to pick our leaders and mentors based on maturity, not their supposed credentials. I often think about the Peanuts gang, and how they did that big Christmas Play together despite their childishness. It would be fun to see those characters grown up, but they were lovable the way they were, as well. (A Charlie Brown Christmas, 1965, Charles Shultz.)

Can we love each other and still realize there is room to improve? I think so.

15. "Just Grow Up"

Have you ever heard the mom of a wayward child say,

"I wish he would just grow up?" What does she mean by that? It's often not said about a small child, but rather someone that should have shown more adult-like traits by now. See? We know deep down what grown-up should look like. The truth is, some of us have hidden behind scriptures hoping the Lord does not notice how immature we are.

I am amazed at the different perspectives people have on growing. Some believe you grow through trials. That could be their experience, but not everyone grows through trials. Some choose not to grow and become bitter in the process.

We sometimes alternate between wondering if hypocrites really do go to church and defending our brethren in an intentional blindness without facing the truth about what is really going on.

I know from God's point of view, grown-up is not as simple as claiming a scripture about who-we-are-in-Christ

Too many people have secured a piece of paper with the education they supposedly needed, but do not yes possess God's qualifications, to oversee others.

I leave you with this thought;

"Let perseverance finish its' work so that you may be mature and complete, not lacking anything." James 1:4. (NIV).

16. How I study

While this would take an entire book to explain, and someone has suggested I write that very book. I will share with you however, some highlights about my studying journey, and how I get my revelations from God.

1. I ask God to speak to me what he wants me to know right now. I see him as my Father, mentor, and friend.

2. I do not assume what he is going to say will be in my bible word-for-word, however there will likely be something in there that backs up what I am hearing.

3. I allow God to teach me through visuals such as trees, lakes, flowers, dogs, people, and other methods he might wish to use.

4. I pray constantly to be a lover of truth.

5. I pray to receive and do all he has for me, while I am upon this earth. I want to be all he ever desired for me to be, in Him.

6. I intentionally assume I do not know everything, yet.

7. I believe there are facets to his word, and what it means to use one time, a passage can mean something else to us at a different time in our walk.

8. I believe the word of God is both seed (an individual concept) and water for that seed at the same time.

9. I believe in chewing on and meditation on a passage until he shows me what he wants me to show me about that passage.

10. I do keep a journal and take notes on what God is showing me, believing if I am faithful to what he said by writing it down, he will reveal more to me.

11. I do not demand for him to teach me what I want to learn, I stay committed to learning what he would like me to know next.

12. I do grab myself by the shirt and make myself study, if I see too many days going by when I haven't.

13. I pray against the yeast of the Pharisee and ask God to produce fruit in my life by his power.

14. I often start with Matthew 5 when I am not sure what to study. Many times, when I start there, the Lord will guide me to something else, as a result.

15. I continually lay aside what I think I know, understanding that if I am not willing to learn and keep on growing, I will not be able to help anyone else.

16. I study anywhere, any time. I have come to recognize this nudge down in my spirit that says, "find out what this means," and respond to that still, small voice.

17. The passage in Romans 8:1 that there is no condemnation to those who are in Christ is the helmet of protection I wear when I study God's word. This is because while I am growing, I cannot afford to let my mind tell me I am doomed every time I see how I am not lining up with God's word at this time.

Conclusion

I hope you've enjoyed this book, as it's been my pleasure to write it. Remember with me please, that we are not here to bash others or make ourselves feel better by pointing out the flaws of our comrades on Planet Earth.

The point has been to be a little humbler, and realize as we look at ourselves, others, and what we've been taught so far in life, perhaps we can get a real passion and hunger and thirst for growing up more in Christ as he intended for us to do.

As 2 Peter 3:18 says, we are all called to grow in Grace and the knowledge of him, our savior, the Lord Jesus Christ.

May we be found faithful in our endeavor to know him, and not fill our lives with empty religious teachings and may Christ be formed within us.

"Father, as my friends who read this come back to you once again seeking to know you, may they have a fresh perspective, by your grace on how to grow in you, Lord." In Jesus' name I pray, amen

References:

NKJV, NIV, KJV Thomas Nelson, www.biblegateway.com

Shultz, Charles, "A Charlie Brown Christmas, 1965

ABOUT THE AUTHOR

Laura attends a Christian University currently and is and avid studier of the bible. Her hunger and thirst for Knowing God began as a teenager and has continued through her lifetime.

Her first book, Grace to the Rescue, details her testimony of coming to Christ, having experienced Lutheran Churches as a child then later, journeying into Independent Charismatic churches, Baptists, and later the Methodist church.

Her quest for answers from God, and resulting revelations are sure to warm your heart, and rain on the seeds God has already planted within you. Contact her at sisterzeal@yahoo.com

CPSIA information can be obtained
at www.ICGtesting.com
Printed in the USA
LVHW051709080419
613378LV00019B/1194/P